MW01264254

The Seven Deadly Sins of Sales

LEIGH BROWN

Mallard Creek Publishing

Mallard Creek Publishing
PO BOX 396
Harrisburg, NC 28075-0396

Limit of Liability/Disclaimer of Warranty:

Publishing and editorial team:
Author Bridge Media, www.AuthorBridgeMedia.com
Project Manager and Editorial Director: Helen Chang
Editor: Jenny Shipley
Publishing Manager: Laurie Aranda
Publishing Assistant: Iris Sasing

Library of Congress Number: 2018902183

ISBN: 978-1-943817-04-7 -- softcover
978-1-943817-05-4 -- hardcover
978-1-943817-08-5 -- ebook
978-1-943817-07-8 -- audiobook

Ordering Information:

DEDICATION

This book is again dedicated to my outrageously authentic family of salespeople, who are reformed sinners like me. May you always remember that your work is critical to preserving the dream, and that you are trusted, admired, and important.

CONTENTS

ACKNOWLEDGMENTS

To all the folks acknowledged in the first book, I still super appreciate you.

Thank you to every client who has ever trusted me with a home purchase or sale. Without your trust in me, neither of these books would have been possible.

To all of the event planners who have asked me to present to your members, agents, and attendees, thank you for the opportunity to share life. I will never take for granted how much you entrust me with the stage.

Thank you to my team members, who continue to make this journey possible every day. Without y'all, I would never have been able to take the stage and find the voice that now encourages others, and I would still be out there committing those deadly sins. You are the best in the industry, and I could not be prouder of each of you for making me look better than I could ever be on my own. I love each of you more than you know.

To Helen Chang, Katherine MacKenett, Julia Watson, and the editorial team at Author Bridge Media, I thank you for helping me turn another book into reality.

To my parents, grandparents, and surrogate family from church, thank you for instilling a strong work ethic in me, allowing my talkativeness and bossiness to create a bigger vision, and loving me. You are not only role models, but also lighthouses by which I guide my own life. I love you all.

To Cora and Timmy, thank you for being patient with your mama traveling and for being the best part of me. I am so proud of you and wish for you to always, always be your authentic, amazing selves that God created so well. I wouldn't wish for anyone except you to be my kids.

To Steve, I'm forever grateful that I found you. Thank you for putting up with this changing, crazy life. You're the calm in my storm. Forever looks amazing with you in the middle of it. I love you.

I am, above all else, a child of God, and I am grateful.

INTRODUCTION

The Crux of the Problem

Sales, as they say, is the oldest profession in the world.

(All right, technically, the oldest profession in the world is prostitution. But that's still sales!)

I kid, but it's safe to say that the sales profession isn't going anywhere anytime soon. Even so, if you're like many of us sales professionals, you've likely seen a bit of a plateau in your business in recent years.

There's just nothing new and exciting happening. And today's customers, frankly, can be downright frustrating to deal with. The average adult's attention span these days is 3.7 seconds, which is why, when you've got a prospect on hold for four minutes and you finally pick up, the person screams at you like he or she has been on hold for four and a half days—that is, *if* the caller waited for you at all.

Customers are people, and people are all too quick to blow things out of proportion. They expect to be catered to in a personalized fashion. They want your attention *now*, whether they've contacted you via phone call, text message, Facebook, Twitter, Instagram, or email. Heck, you probably sleep with your phone under your pillow trying to stay on top of responding to all those little messages coming in from every which way, trying to answer every one of them quickly enough to keep your customers loyal.

Bottom line, consumer expectations are an increasingly difficult-to-hit moving target, more so now than ever before in our lifetimes. The trouble, though, with spending so much time and energy trying to hit that moving target is that it's got us focusing our attention outward instead of where it ought to be directed: inward, right back at our own selves.

We spend our days in reactive mode, putting out fires and feeling exhausted trying to stay on top of it all. Then we wake up the next morning and start the same cycle all over again. This leaves us no time to reflect on our business lives like we do (or try to do) on our personal lives.

We completely lose sight of our professional goals and priorities. Then, just like Pandora of the old Greek myths, with that pretty box of hers, we unleash a whole host of sins on our businesses in the process: the seven deadly sins of sales.

Trust me. We're all guilty of at least some of these. Here's the good news, though: they don't have to hang around haunting us for the rest of our days.

"But Leigh," you say, "I feel stuck in this rut. I'm crazy busy every day, and I feel just plain exhausted. Heck, it's all I can do to just keep going through the motions. How on earth can I even begin to fix this?"

Well, don't you worry. There is a deceptively simple way to root out the seven sins of sales from your life, and I'm here to tell you how to do it.

From Sinner to Saint

Before you can conquer the seven deadly sins of sales, you first have to take a good, long look at what you're doing in your own business. Once you see which of the sins you've been committing, you can take charge of your own behavior and turn it around.

This means approaching the world with a proactive attitude instead of just being reactive. It means starting your day off with a satisfyingly productive task instead of chasing customers around like your hair is on fire. It means learning to embrace conversations with other people instead of hiding from them.

Finally, it means learning to prioritize your business and personal life in a way that will lead to better results on all fronts. And maybe—just maybe—you won't go through that fourth divorce, your kids won't be in therapy, and you can stop smoking a pack a day.

You might still sleep with your phone under your pillow, but now you're just checking your sleep patterns instead of checking Facebook in a panic in the middle of the night.

Most of all, with the fog obscuring your vision now cleared, you can see the big picture again. You're once more focused on your long-term goals and actively moving toward them—meaning, you actually have a chance of achieving them.

Let's be real. You're still going to be frazzled and exhausted, because, frankly, until we fix the way our society works, we're all going to be frazzled and exhausted. At least now, though, you're in a much better mood about it. That's because once you're able to get back on track with your goals and get your priorities sorted, you're going to be genuinely happier with the direction your life and your work are headed.

Think about it like working out. If you don't work out, you feel exhausted because you feel fat and bloated and you've accomplished nothing. After you work out, sure, you feel exhausted, but you also feel energized. Your endorphins are going, and you feel good about having done something good for yourself.

The same principle applies when you're finally living sales sin–free. You know you're doing something wonderful for yourself and your business, and you can feel it. You'll find your attitude will perk right up.

And that truly makes all the difference.

The "No Bullshit" Realtor®

My clients have dubbed me the "No Bullshit" Realtor®. They know I can be counted on to call things the way I see them, whether I'm selling them a house or calling someone out for those white pumps after Labor Day.

Throughout my life, I've worked in all kinds of sales, from waiting tables and bartending, to being a stockbroker, to selling insurance for Prudential and chainsaws for Husqvarna. In 2000, I joined my Daddy in real estate, and we built a business together.

Before we knew it, we'd bought a franchise with RE/MAX and experienced great success . . . until the downturn hit in 2007.

Suddenly, instead of buying new houses, our clients were trying to figure out how to continue to afford their existing homes or how to get out from being underwater as quickly and gracefully as possible. They didn't need fluff and puff. They needed someone who could get down to business and ask the tough questions about money and financial habits.

That's what we did. We modified the way we did business to focus on finding the best solution for each family. The conversations we had on the way there weren't pretty, but people walked out of my office knowing I'd meant every word that had come out of my mouth. "Leigh will tell it to you straight," they said. "She won't bullshit you. She's the real deal."

That period of time wasn't easy. But my Daddy and I shared the belief that we could help people if we were honest with them. Our clients just needed someone to help them take a long, hard look at the situation they'd gotten themselves into and identify and sort through the best solutions. Our commitment to being straight shooters got us and them through it.

Not only did we help hundreds and hundreds of families, but our business actually grew while others faltered. This is how my team wound up in the *Wall Street Journal*'s list of the top 150 real estate teams.

Today, I speak to thousands of people every year on the power of authenticity and the seven deadly sins of sales. I also reach thousands more online through Facebook, Twitter, and Instagram. I'm the author of *Outrageous Authenticity* and a contributor to several different industry news sources. I have appeared on NPR, HGTV, and CNBC, and I've been featured in the *New York Times*, the *Wall Street Journal*, and *Money Magazine*, among other publications.

I'm a RE/MAX and REALTORS Political Action Committee (RPAC) hall-of-famer. I've earned the RE/MAX Circle of Legends award, and I've been listed on the *Wall Street Journal*'s REAL Trends US Top 200 team more than once. Most importantly, my clients still call me the "No Bullshit" Realtor®, because I'm still actively representing buyer and seller clients.

Do you know how I got here? And, more importantly, how I've *stayed* here?

By taking my own medicine! Y'all aren't the only ones committing the seven deadly sins. I am a

backslider too. Yet I have seen the light, and so will
you. Just you keep reading.

 "If you go beyond this point, you're
going to get your feelings hurt. But
it'll be worth it! Cross my heart."

How to Get the Most out of This Book

I have been a Realtor® for almost twenty years and
am fully aware of how the seven deadly sins of sales
can affect me and my business. But these sins are
not relevant exclusively to real estate professionals.
These sins apply to sales professionals throughout
every industry—and to each one of us as human
beings.

So back to the state of your reactive, overworked,
going-through-the-motions self. How are you going
to get yourself out of the mess you're in?

Well, first things first: you're going to strap yourself in and leave your ego at the door. (Spoiler alert:
that's Sin #1!) You're gonna understand that you're
about to have your toes stepped on, so put on your

steel-toed boots. Yep, you're about to be called up in front of the priest, in front of God and everybody for what you've been doing wrong. That means you need to sit still and read this book from start to finish to learn about every one of these seven deadly sins.

Oh, you'll *think* that you're not committing them—that is, until after you've read about them and had a minute to sit and reflect on each one. That's when you'll realize that, yeah, there's room for improvement in all of us.

That means y'all need to read each chapter and sit with it. Take a long, hard look at yourself and your business, and adjust *one thing* related to each sin you find yourself guilty of. Then move on to the next sin, and adjust one more thing. Before you know it, you'll be done reading this book, and you'll have tweaked and fine-tuned a few things here or there.

Each of these small changes won't seem like much at the time. But taken together as a whole, that's going to be seven steps exponentially better than where you were before.

Face the Music

It's time to face the music, and I'll be with you every step of the way, helping to lighten your load with a little of my trademark *Outrageously Authentic* humor to help the medicine go down.

By the time we're done, by God, it'll be worth it. You'll feel healthier, happier, and more present in the time you spend with your loved ones. You'll be more profitable. And what's more, this is how we change the perception of salespeople in every industry, *forever*.

You know what that means? People will like you again! You'll be invited to parties that don't involve buying stuff. If you're single, when people see that your Tinder profile says you're in sales, they'll swipe right. You'll get to go to the "ten items or less" line, even if you have twelve items. You get the picture.

If you commit to addressing these things within your business and your personal life, you're going to see results within thirty days—no lie.

It's going to sound simple to solve these issues— and really, it is. You just have to do the work. Clearing the seven deadly sins of sales out of your life is like working out. It sounds easy to put on your shoes and go for a walk, but still, people don't do it. You have to take the time to self-reflect and know what you need to do better. Then you've got to take steps to make it happen.

Once you've put in this groundwork, then even if you happen to backslide into bad habits now and then, you'll be able to catch yourself and get back to where you need to be. Even better, you'll do it quicker the next time, because you'll be an old hand at all of this by then.

Are you ready to go from sinner to saint? Then hop aboard, y'all. It's going to be one helluva ride.

Chapter 1

The Seven Deadly Sins of Sales

The Seven Deadly *What* Now?

Let's get one thing clear right up front: the seven deadly sins of sales are a sight different from your good old traditional seven deadlies. We're not going to be talking about your gluttonous or lecherous ways in this book, y'all. You can deal with those on your own!

When it comes to the seven deadly sins of sales, we're honestly just talking habitual mistakes we all make as salespeople.

Now, I know that folks—me included—don't like to be told they're making a mistake, because no one enjoys feeling like a screw-up. Committing a sin, however, is something you don't always realize you're in control of. Sinning, you see, is often simply a matter of poor discipline.

The goal here is to re-create a new and *different* kind of habitual discipline, one specifically designed to keep you from committing these particular seven deadly sins. That's what this book is all about.

Getting right with this new level of discipline is what's going to make the key difference in your business. We're talking about the difference between making merely enough income to subsist as a salesperson and making the rock-star, six-figure income you heard about back when you first had stars in your eyes over the idea of living a commission-based lifestyle.

You know what lifestyle I'm talking about. It's the one you read about in that first Craigslist ad that promised you $100,000 in your first year. Yes, you fell for that ad—you know you did! And then you actually got into sales and found out it's a whole lot harder than anybody told you.

The reality is that it's hard to know what you're doing well and what you're doing wrong in our profession, because there's not a great mentor or apprenticeship system out there. I mean, you know how to do *some* things, and you might be doing them moderately okay. But surely you could be doing some things better, don't you think?

No one wants to be mediocre, but if you're letting the seven deadly sins of sales flourish in your business, mediocrity is where you'll stay. If you want to be *super*, well then you've got to get back on the wagon. And you've got to practice exercising your new discipline until it simply becomes second nature.

The Path to Redemption

So if we're not talking gluttony and lechery, what exactly *are* the seven deadly sins of sales?

The chapters ahead will break them down for you one by one. We'll discuss what each sin is and what kind of problems it creates in your business. I'll also teach you simple strategies and tricks you can use to develop the discipline you'll need to banish that sin from your business *and* your life.

Before we launch into Sin #1 in the next chapter, let's take a quick look at all the sins together so you have a sense of the territory we'll be covering from here on out.

Sin #1: "I" syndrome (Ego over substance).
There's a reason this is the number one

sin—because if you count the number of times you say the word "I" in the course of a single day, presentation, or phone call, you'll realize exactly why people are tired of talking to you. Stop letting your ego sabotage you! In this chapter, I'll help you reconnect with how to talk *to* people and not at them.

Sin #2: *The morning after (Abandonment).* Yes, yes, I know you meant to call those past clients and talk to the people who did business with you once upon a time. The path to hell is paved with good intentions, as they say. And the path to redemption is paved with working those contacts and clients you spent so much time and effort winning over in the first place!

Sin #3: Settle down, Francis (Misplaced *sense of urgency).* This is the sin of acting like your hair is on fire at all times. However, there are few situations for which you should have your hair set on fire. We'll discuss when to grant a situation a high sense of urgency and when to dunk your head in the tub and settle down.

Sin #4: My, that's a high horse you've got there (Cherry-picking). Cherry-picking is strategically—or *not* so strategically—deciding with whom you will or won't do business. Not only does this possibly put you in conflict with federal and state laws, but it can also destroy your business if your particular selection of clients suddenly fails to perform.

Sin #5: Fish or cut bait (Aversion to loss). Learning not to cherry-pick with whom to work is one thing, but being afraid or unable to remove a poisonous person from your life is something entirely different. Yes, you'll give folks a fair shot, but if it turns out they can't behave themselves, then you have got to learn when and how to cut your losses and move on.

Sin #6: Cut the bullhockey (Fluff and puff). This is not 1985. Glamour, my friends, is gone. Today's consumers don't want a false fantasy; they want facts. It's not just time to tell the truth; it's time to understand that telling the truth is the most powerful sales tool you have.

Sin #7: Put your horse before the damn cart already (Inverted priorities). We all know we're supposed to put God and family before business. However, salespeople have a bad habit of putting business first, because if they're not selling, they're not getting paid. It's not long before "it's only one phone call" or "it's just this one delay" can turn into you letting your life pass you by without actually living it. And *that* is the real tragedy here.

And finally, we'll wrap up with a good hard look at how to put your new discipline into practice at the next level: by building stronger relationships with everyone in your life, from your clients and your teammates to your family.

Confession Is Good for the Soul

Remember when I said that you weren't alone in committing the seven deadly sins of sales?

Yeah. My name is Leigh Brown. And I, too, have sinned.

I was never good at typical networking—you know, the cocktail-hour thing. But I have always been good at reading, absorbing, and understanding how data affect an environment. That's why my sales continue to increase, no matter what's happening in the market—because I work to make sure I understand the overall schematics.

When I started seeing other sales professionals making the same mistakes over and over again and hurting their businesses in the process, I couldn't help but start to put two and two together and shake my head. "Mmm mmm," I said. "Look at Jane. She's fluff-and-puffing it even worse than ol' Hank down at the car dealership."

And yep, you guessed it. It wasn't long before I realized *I* was making some of those same mistakes myself. Not only that, but even since I've remedied them, I've still fallen off the wagon of good habits from time to time, just like everybody else.

Look. Nobody's perfect. But if we suck up our pride a little and commit to being the best version of ourselves we can possibly be, we can kick these seven deadlies to the curb where they belong. And if we do happen to fall off the wagon every now and then, we'll know exactly how to pick ourselves up, dust off the dirt, and get right back up there.

And speaking of sucking it up, our first stop along the way is a timely reminder that there's no "I" in "team."

Chapter 2

Sin 1: "I" Syndrome (Ego over Substance)

It's Not You, It's Me

Let's talk about where you are in your sales career today. And let's say you're in real estate, specifically, just as an example.

I'm willing to bet that when you first went into real estate, it wasn't just for the money or the so-called flexible hours. (Ha! So flexible you get to work *all* of them.) No, I'll wager that back then you had a genuine desire to provide a better real estate experience for your consumers—to be there to hold their hand through an incredibly stressful series of financial decisions that will affect the rest of their lives.

After working in this profession for many years, however, you've probably had an experience such as this one: You've gone to an appointment where you're so bored by that same neighborhood, the same basic floor plan, and those cookie-cutter houses, because you've sold that same style five times in a row. You have basically been dealing with that same house your entire career, and you don't get excited about it anymore because of one simple thing . . .

You've forgotten the real reason you're a salesperson.

You've forgotten that this home is your client's single largest financial instrument. And that it belongs to an individual who is unique.

It might not be that big of a deal to *you*. You do this every single day. But you've lost sight of the fact that this is a huge deal to your clients. If you can always keep in mind the reason you got into real estate—or any type of sales—it will make it much easier to engage authentically with every client you come into contact with.

That reason you went into sales? It was at least in part to help people make the right decision, to make a positive impact in other people's lives. So, for goodness' sake, act like it!

Find Your "Why" Again

In order to be successful in sales, you have to do one thing before anything else, every single day, and that is to get the hell out of your own way.

And what is the best way to do that?

It's to reconnect with your *why*.

Why did *you*, specifically, go into your sales career? Why do you still do it today? If you can find a way to re-engage with this sense of purpose, you will be that much more successful, because your actions and your connections with the people you serve will be purpose driven. And boy, does that show. It is not a thing you can fake, believe me.

"I" syndrome happens when you've got your ego where your heart should be. When you shift the focus to substance over ego, however, you're no longer talking *at* people; you're talking *with* them. Once you take yourself out of the equation, you're better able to find out what's actually important to the person you're talking to. You're better able to convey to that person why you do what you do, and why you might be the correct choice for his or her needs at this time, so you can both reach a mutually beneficial outcome.

If, on the other hand, you let your "I" syndrome go untreated and put ego before substance, people can smell it on you a mile away. And they just plain don't want to hear it. It's the same as posting a dating profile on Match.com that only brags about your accomplishments, rather than talking about a single damn thing you actually care about. Honestly, who wants that? Newsflash: nobody.

Now, over time, your *why* might migrate a bit from point A to point B. That's only natural as we get older and our priorities shift. But that's no excuse to lose sight of why you do what you do in the first place.

Keep your eye on your *why* and you keep your eye on the big prize: a purpose-driven career that leads to a purpose-driven life.

How to Bring Purpose Back into Your Work

"Now, Leigh," you're going to say, "it's one thing to remember why I got into this profession in the first place, but what can I actually *do* to demonstrate that I'm in touch with that?"

I am so glad you asked. I have two tips for you that will help you connect more authentically and substantively with each and every person you interact with in your work.

Define Your Value Proposition

You can start by defining your value proposition.

Sales professionals today face incredible competition—not just from each other, but from technology platforms that offer consumers an ever-expanding array of options for how and from whom to buy what they need. Even so, the only way all these competitors can take our business from us is if we lose sight of what it is we provide to the people who entrust us with their financial decisions.

Defining your value proposition starts with knowing your strengths and your *why*. What is the unique benefit you bring your customers based on those two things? Something that might help you figure this out is to stop and answer this question: What part of what you do are you the most passionate and excited about?

For me, it's that I get my jollies out of helping the consumer navigate the minefield of real estate. I genuinely enjoy managing that process, even though I know it's never going to go perfectly. My clients know that we might both get blown up crossing that minefield, but if we do, we're damn well going to get blown up together. And we're going to cross that finish line together too—even if I have to carry them over it while the boom box plays "Eye of the Tiger" behind us.

Discover your own value proposition. Distill it down to its core essence. Once you know this and you can concisely convey it to consumers, you can defeat any website or any other competitor that rears its head in the marketplace.

Get Personal

Step two is to ditch the platitudes and spam emails and get personal.

For example, if you're a real estate agent, maybe you're responding to incoming inquiries with some generic email that says, "Thank you for visiting my website. I'd love to set you up on a VIP home search to look at properties that fit your needs in today's market."

Put yourself in the consumer's shoes. If you receive that as a reply to an inquiry, is that going to make you want to respond to that agent? No!

Think about what consumers actually want to see, not just what *you* want them to see. You'll never know what people really need unless you communicate on a personal level.

Key Takeaways for a Substance-Driven Career

Once you achieve a substance-driven approach to sales, you'll make more money, you'll be happier, and your clients and customers will seek you out time and time again *and* refer you to their friends.

Even so, figuring out why you do what you do and encapsulating it can certainly be challenging, considerably more so than tackling the rest of the sins in this book. To that end, here are some things you can try to get yourself started:

- Think about the last five deals you closed. Why did those clients choose you? What did they say about you at the end of the process? This is perhaps your best resource for uncovering your *why*. Put together your elevator speech based on these people's belief in you.

- Then work on your value proposition. What is it about your *why* that makes you stand out from your competitors? Think about why *you* are the correct person to meet consumers' needs. Then distill that down into a simple benefits statement for them. What can you offer them that other sales pros in your industry can't?

- Read Simon Sinek's powerful book *Start with Why*, or even just the first few chapters. It is a testament to the power of discovering your purpose and using that as a springboard to inspire yourself and others around you.

- Another thing that might help? If you're having trouble with your *why* and you haven't read my first book, pick up a copy of *Outrageous Authenticity*. It's guaranteed to

help get you back in touch with whatever
it is that makes you *you*.

Once you've got your "I" syndrome wrangled and your substance up at the forefront of your business where it should be, you're ready to tackle Sin #2: the wham, bam, thank you ma'am of sales sins.

Chapter 3

Sin 2: The Morning After (Abandonment)

The Power of the Impactful Gesture

Several years ago, I found myself in a bit of a pickle with my business. We were looking for a way to reconnect with and appreciate our past clients—*in person*. After all, that's how you get repeat business and referrals and create stronger ties with your community.

We'd tried offering them free pies right before Thanksgiving if they'd only swing by our office, but that was a bust. People didn't want a free pie enough to drive across town for one.

As luck would have it, around this time my daughter joined an audition choir that sells Fraser fir wreaths during the holidays to raise money to keep kids involved in the arts. I remember when we first brought one of these wreaths home: it smelled amazing, it was beautifully made, and we got to decorate it as a family before we hung it on the door. It was so special and so satisfying to know that the money went to such a good cause.

That's when it hit me. What if I bought a hundred of these wreaths to support local children in the arts? Then my staff and I could pick the hundred clients we most appreciated—our diamonds, as we like to call them—get in the car, and hand deliver a wreath to each of their doorsteps.

The response was simply amazing.

My client base is made of Christian, Jewish, Hindu, Buddhist, atheist, and Muslim folks. We've got a little bit of everybody, and every single one of our clients was just as delighted as could be to get a visit, a hug, and a fresh fir wreath to decorate (or not!) as they pleased.

We made a tradition of it. To this day, we get handwritten thank-you notes and posts and pictures on social media of decorated wreaths from these clients. It makes exactly the kind of impact we wanted. Our clients love it and look forward to "wreath day." We get to support kids and the local economy, because the wreaths come from a locally owned tree farm. And we get the ongoing personal interaction with clients we were hoping for.

It doesn't get better than that, friends.

The Lost Opportunity

Going and hand delivering those wreaths every year is an example of the *opposite* of the second deadly sin of sales: abandonment, or what I like to call "the morning after."

The best way to explain this sin is to use another example. This time, let's go with dating. Say you've got a date with a handsome guy whom you think could be "The One."

You fix yourself up and put on that cute new outfit you bought to create the best first impression. Then he picks you up and opens the car door for you, and you have the most wonderful date. You ask and answer questions and tell each other all of your funny stories. The end of this perfect night comes, and you get that magical first kiss at your doorstep when he drops you off back home.

And then . . . he never calls you again.

Yes, that is a record scratch you hear in your head. And it's the same sound your clients hear when, after having held their hand for three months through a complicated and difficult sales process, you get your commission and they never hear from *you* ever again.

You know you've been guilty of this one. We've all done it. Many of us still do. But this sin comes at the price of wasted opportunities. Because our clients have to remember that, hey, *we still exist*, in order to bring us their return business or send us their friends, it's vital that you make the effort to keep in touch with them after a deal closes.

Staying connected to clients you've done good work for leads to more business—from them and from their friends, family, and colleagues. Why not continue that relationship and put that hard-won trust and goodwill to work for you?

If you do this with *all* your good clients, suddenly they become your biggest source of new business, because they know who you are, what you do, and what *you specifically* have to offer. And they'll tell anyone they meet who needs someone with your expertise.

Fail to keep up those relationships and, a few years down the line when that client decides to make an upgrade, he or she will have forgotten your name, your number, your very existence. When that happens, you'll have only yourself to blame. You're spending time and resources trying to drum up new business that you could have gotten today for free if you'd only stop abandoning people after the first date.

How to Stay Connected

The last thing you want to do is lose out on business because you've abandoned your customers. Here are a few strategies I use to stay connected and develop impactful relationships with my clients.

Track Your Information

First, you need a good customer relationship management (CRM) system. This can be as simple as an Excel spreadsheet. Honest to God, that's all you need in many cases.

A good CRM system is critical, because if you don't have your customers' contact information, you can't stay in touch.

For each client you come into contact with, list in your database a name, address, phone number, email address, and note to tell you where that client came from (e.g., a specific advertising platform, a social media site, an event, or another client). This last field is especially important, because it allows you to track, over time, where your business is actually coming from. This is how you identify your diamonds—like the clients I take those wreaths to every holiday season.

Remember: you need this information, but bottom line, it's not doing you any good if you don't use it.

Make Visits (Yes, in Person)

This one is going to be very shocking, but go visit people. Have physical conversations with them, and leave your phone in the car so neither you nor the person you're talking to will be distracted when it inevitably buzzes.

Social media is great, but it's no substitution for standing in front of your clients and looking them in the eye while you talk to them. The lost art of communication is lost only if we let it be. Use personal communication to your advantage, because, Lord knows, a large majority of your competition won't bother with it in this day and age—to their own peril.

Stay in Touch with Video

Video is not an excuse to skip in-person visits! Realistically, though, there's only one of you, so sending clients a video of yourself at least once a month—through email or social media—is a great way to stay in touch in between those more personal individual visits.

You have only about ten seconds to grab someone's attention in your video, so start off with a good hook. Also make sure to talk about things that actually make an impact. Maybe discuss something related to a product you sold them. Has there been a relevant recent change or technological breakthrough? Or something else they need to know?

Your video can also include updates about things you're doing that they might be interested in, like community outreach or local events you'll be attending, where they can connect with you in person.

Key Takeaways for Staying in Touch

If you're looking to improve your track record for staying connected, you can start with these points:

- Take twenty minutes to re-evaluate your current outreach strategy. Are you making the kind of impact you want with your clients, or is it time to try something different?

- Are you practicing good CRM? When was the last time you updated your database with the information of the people who have contacted you this week, this month, or this year? Likewise, when was the last time you went through your list to analyze where your business is actually coming from?

- Once you've identified your diamonds, what are you doing to continue to cultivate those relationships (personal visits, social media, videos, emails, etc.)?

Next up, we're on to Sin #3: the fine art of knowing when something is truly urgent and when you just need to settle down!

Chapter 4

Sin 3: "Settle Down, Francis!" (Misplaced Sense of Urgency)

The Real Reason Business Is Slow

The third of our seven deadly sins of sales is having no sense of urgency.

When it comes to this one, I like to do a little experiment when I travel. In each city, I go to at least eight different local Realtor® websites. I pick these at random, and then I enter my information using a fake name and a disguised email address.

That way, they have no idea that it was Leigh Brown on their website.

Every once in a blue moon, I will get more than one call back or, much more likely, a spam email inviting me to an open house. But you know what I get from the majority?

Crickets.

That's right. No call. No email. Nothing.

Salespeople like to blame the competition—other people and new tech platforms alike—for taking their business. But for many of us, we need look no further than our own lack of anything resembling a sense of urgency.

We have gotten downright lazy, y'all.

Don't make excuses for yourself. If you are in sales and you get a call from a number you don't recognize, you don't have the luxury of assuming it's a wrong number or a telemarketer. Do that and you might as well literally be throwing leads in the trash.

If you want more business? Well, for starters, answer your dadgum phone!

Settle Down, Francis!

Unfortunately, our industry's problems with urgency aren't limited to not having enough of it. Sometimes the issue is just the opposite—something you might know as "hair on fire" syndrome. This is when someone doesn't know what to do, because he or she is just running around like the proverbial chicken with its head cut off, waiting for someone to say, "Settle down, Francis!"

Being successful in sales requires a balanced sense of urgency. So it's imperative that sales professionals learn to tell the difference between what is actually urgently important and what can wait twenty minutes or an hour or a day to be solved in a rational and reasonable manner.

What happens when your sense of urgency goes off-kilter is that you lose all sense of priorities, and that just destroys your ability to make good decisions. You get so bogged down dealing with the small stuff that you ignore the big stuff you should be paying attention to—like, hey, oops, when you really *are* on fire. Then, instead of solving the challenges that come your way, you end up creating bigger problems for yourself than the ones you started out with.

On the flip side, a healthy sense of urgency leads to a timely, measured, and sane response to your clients, coworkers, and prospects. Your priorities are in order. Your mind is calm. And you can get on with your day in an organized and professional manner, rising to the challenge of whatever obstacles you're presented with instead of shrieking and running the other way.

Once you deal with any—real or imagined—fires currently in your hair, you can slow down enough to pay attention to all the things that matter. So what's the number one way to stay on top of a proper sense of urgency?

It's easier than you think!

How to Prioritize Like a Champ

There are plenty of tips and tricks you can use to learn how to be a master when it comes to prioritizing your time. Here are a few of my favorites.

Separate Your RP from Your NRP

One of the single most useful strategies I've found for prioritizing work tasks is to make two separate lists of all the things I have to do every week. One set of these activities gets sorted under RP activities. That stands for Revenue-Producing. These are the things that are truly going to drive your future business, and they should be your highest priority.

The other list you'll make is for your NRP, or Non-Revenue-Producing, activities. This includes things like your Facebook outreach, emails, texts, and sending out marketing materials.

Successful salespeople know that the NRPs have to wait until the RPs are done. Deconstruct your day and your week. Divide up everything you do into either RP or NRP. Then, within those two groups, assign priority to those tasks accordingly. If it's an NRP and it's not time sensitive, it goes to the bottom of that list. If it's an RP and it *is* time sensitive? Yep. Straight to the top of that list.

Hire a Team

One of the main reasons salespeople develop "hair on fire" syndrome is sheer burnout. You're so overwhelmed with work tasks that you can't possibly stay on top of everything, and, as a result, you spend all your time trying to put out fires instead of getting out in front of them before they start.

If this describes you, perhaps it's high time you hired some help. An administrative professional can help you with things like social media management, outbound marketing, keeping up with emails and phone messages, and managing your database.

Are you starting to see a pattern here? I bet you are. These tasks all fall under the non-revenue-producing category, leaving you freed up to focus on your RPs. What a concept!

Key Takeaways for Keeping an Even Keel

Cultivating a proper sense of urgency allows you to stay organized and project a professional, put-together image to everyone you interact with. Here are a few suggestions to root out this particular sin:

- Contact a handful of random sales professionals in your field. You'll learn a ton about what to do and what not to do. You might even find people doing what you do *so well* that you learn something from them that you can emulate in your own business.

- Track how you're spending your time on work tasks. For a full week, keep a diary or a spreadsheet of how you actually spend your time at work. This will give you a breakdown of time spent on RPs versus NRPs.

- Read *Eat That Frog!* by Brian Tracy, my favorite book on how to stop procrastinating and improve your productivity. It'll help you zero in on any bad habits you've developed that are keeping you from getting things done.

Now that you've learned how to get yourself organized and keep your cool, we're ready to move on to the next sin: prancin' around on that high horse of yours by cherry-picking whom you will and won't work with.

Chapter 5

Sin 4: My, That's a High Horse You've Got There (Cherry-Picking)

Snobbery Equals Death

In 2015, I listed a house for $8,000. Yes, that was the list price, not my fee! I told the seller, "We should donate it to Habitat for Humanity." He tried, but Habitat *said no*.

Well, we found a buyer, and when we were sitting at the closing table, I asked my client the question you should always ask twice in every transaction. At the time of listing, you say, "Why me?" Your client will tell you the pretty answer that time, describing the positive first impression you gave, because you're still on your first date.

At the closing table, though, it's a different story. This is a later stage in the relationship. Now your bed-head and morning breath are no longer a secret. But your client didn't get scared out of bed at 8:00 a.m. and, instead, stayed there with you. So now you can ask "Why me?" again and get a deeper answer.

In this particular case, the client with the $8,000 house said, "Well, frankly, I wasn't going to call you, Leigh Brown."

I said, "Aw, why not?"

"I figured you'd be too busy for this little house," he said.

And I said, "I'm never too busy for you."

"Well, I know that *now*," he told me.

He had called six other real estate agents, y'all. And every one of them told him that it was not enough of a house to mess with. Right then and there, I apologized to him on behalf of everybody in this profession.

Now, I have sold some multimillion-dollar properties, but they're no more valuable to me than my $8,000 client, who, by the way, owns a pretty nice personal home.

Guess whom he's going to list it with in the spring?

That's right. Leigh Brown. The asking price for that one? Let's just say it's several of those $8,000 houses.

I bet those other six Realtors® who couldn't be bothered to work with this client would surely be kicking themselves now if they realized the opportunity they missed.

Get Off Your High Horse

Cherry-picking is very rarely the sin of the brand new, hungry, aggressive salesperson who chases every single opportunity. No, this is the sin you start committing after you find some measure of success. Your phone is ringing every day. You have clients who are using you consistently. You've begun to develop a tendency to pick and choose with whom you work.

This can be a positive thing for your business, or it can be the worst business decision you've ever made.

Case in point? Those six Realtors® who refused to work with my client's little house.

The reality is that a sales career is built almost entirely on relationships. Because of this, when you pick and choose your clients based on limited information, you're running a risk of closing yourself off to a new business relationship that could prove incredibly valuable over the long term.

When you tell someone you can't or won't work for that person because "that's not the price range I serve," what you're saying is that you're too important for such a measly commission. In doing so, you're not just being rude. You're failing to honor the fact that you even received the call in the first place.

The consequences for this behavior don't stop at losing that person's current and future business.

People who feel they've been treated poorly by you don't live in a vacuum. They have a network of friends, family members, colleagues, and other folks to whom they talk on a regular basis—more than likely on social media. And instead of creating raving fans who love working with you, you've just created disgruntled people who are going to go to their network—or worse, Yelp—and say, "Ugh. Don't bother calling So-and-So. He won't even return your calls."

On the other hand, you can choose to take those incoming calls, answer people's questions respectfully, and learn a little about what it is they need—both now and looking forward to the future. And what if you choose to take the job, even if the deal isn't exactly what you are looking for? These people will sing your praises up and down the block. They will be your customers for life. And as their fortunes rise or fall, they will invite you along for the ride by continuing to give you their business and telling everyone they know how much they love you.

And that is why cherry-picking is more often than not a terrible way to do business.

Diversification—Not Just for Your Stock Portfolio!

Another thing to consider is what can happen if you cultivate just one particular demographic for your client list. Think about this for just a minute. What happens when the market for that group takes a bad turn?

We saw this big time in real estate between 2007 and 2013. Prior to those dark years, there were a ton of real estate agents who would say, "I only work the luxury market," or "I only work golf course properties." They were so specific in their high-end niches.

When the market turned, those parts of the market died first.

Those people found themselves out of work fast, because they had developed a habit of telling people that they were too good to work less expensive properties. Or they were too busy to help somebody who was smaller. Bottom line, they did not have the kind of diversified business that allows for long-term success.

Diversification is something you need in your client base when you're in sales. There's never been a recession, depression, or any other kind of economic epoch where the markets died 100 percent. That's because when you hit different market conditions, there are still some products that will always be bought and sold. Sure, some pockets get quieter than others, but sales continue to happen.

So you'd better make sure you have clients in multiple pockets to see you through tough times.

Key Takeaways to Honor Every Client

Always remember that, when somebody who represents a low-level commission calls you, the person called you because of your positive reputation. It is a compliment when someone seeks you out. Here are some things you can do to help yourself honor that:

- Check your ego at the door. If you need a refresher course in this one, go back and visit the lessons learned when dealing with Sin #1: Ego over substance.

- Answer your phone. Call people back. And most importantly, ask them questions. This not only honors the person you're talking to, but it allows you to collect the information you need to make a good decision about working with that person. Also, read *Permission Marketing: Turning Strangers into Friends, and Friends into Customers* by Seth Godin. It's a gold mine of information about how best to utilize this winning strategy.

- And finally, if after getting more information you determine you *are* going to cherry-pick this one, do it respectfully. Say something like, "You've just offered me a great opportunity. However, I just don't have the bandwidth right now to take care of you in the way you deserve to be handled. So let me recommend another professional I trust with my overflow business." And then actually give the prospective client the name and phone number of a great competitor who fits that bill.

Learning how *not* to shoot yourself in the foot by cherry-picking is one thing, but it's an entirely different sin to continue working with a problem client after he or she has proven to be more trouble than he or she is worth. In the next chapter, we'll talk about the fifth deadly sin of sales: not knowing when to cut bait.

Chapter 6

Sin 5: Fish or Cut Bait (Aversion to Loss)

A Step Too Far

In the last chapter, we learned the perils of cherry-picking your clients. All of that said, I want to be very careful in differentiating those situations from working with toxic people.

As an example, I once listed a house for a fellow we'll call Fred. Now Fred was fairly crass and aggressive. I'm tough, so I thought, "Okay, he's no charmer. But I can suck it up for a few months and get this house sold."

The house itself was no problem at all. It was a nice home: good price point, well kept, easy to show. This was before the downturn, so the market was solid.

Sure enough, we quickly got an offer on the house. What I didn't know at the time was that Fred had been going across the street and spying on the property while I showed it. When I called him later to tell him about the offer—which was really good, by the way—and how excited I was about it, he said, "I'm not selling to *those people*."

"What do you mean, 'those people'?" I asked. "It's a Veterans Affairs (aka VA) loan. They've got the paperwork all signed. Numbers are good, the dates look good. What's the problem?"

"I'm not selling my house to those kind of people," he said.

At that point, I figured out what he meant. As you, too, may have surmised, Fred was from a different cultural and racial background than these buyers. He had decided he wasn't going to sell to them based on that.

Well, I have zero place in my life for bigots. So I fired him on the spot.

He protested that I couldn't fire him—until I showed him the clause in my listing agreement that says either party can unilaterally terminate the agreement at any time. So I called my clause into effect and told Fred I'd give the buyers' agent his contact information and have the agent call him directly to present their offer. "I am not representing somebody who's going to behave this way," I told him. Fred actually hired a lawyer and tried to sue me for firing him. It was a lost case before it even began because of that clause in my listing agreement.

The moral of this story? Everyone deserves a fair shot, but life is too short to work with jacklegs.

Cut Your Losses

Up to the point when I fired him, I'd been stomaching Fred's lesser bad behavior for nearly three months, as I stood to make a commission of somewhere in the ballpark of nine grand from the sale of his house. There comes a point, however, when no amount of money is worth the aggravation of working with someone who is making your life miserable.

When I realized the extent to which this client was an overgrown man-baby incapable of behaving like a civil, rational adult, I was done.

There are times in your professional life when you will add up the pros and cons of working with someone you don't like and decide to grin and bear it. At those times, you lean into being the kind of person your grandma taught you to be—with her wonderful manners and her church gloves. You manage to get the job done as gracefully as possible.

And then there are times when you realize someone is genuinely not worth the spike in your blood pressure that happens every time you talk to him or her. In times like these, you don't lean into what Grandma taught you. You take those gloves off, lean into your inner tough guy, stand your ground, and define your boundaries. Sometimes it's better to let a bad client or a bad deal go than to chase a few stray dollars.

As salespeople, we spend most of our lives looking for approval, so it can be all too easy to fall into the trap of working with abusive clients. But when you continue to invite these people to do business with you, you can't act surprised when they call you up at midnight and scream at you and cuss you out. When you say, "I'm asleep," they say, "Well, if you want my business, you will be available 24/7!"

These are the clients who will destroy you. We've all had them. Either we try to make them like us, or we hide from them because we can't handle one more nasty phone call. But the last thing we ever do is cut them loose.

Once you do learn to cut 'em loose, though, it is a *revelation*. Suddenly, you can breathe easily again. You can sleep through the night in peace. You find you have more time to work with genuinely nice, delightful people—the clients you had nothing left to give to because you were so worn out working with Freds.

For your own sake, learn to fire people! You'll be amazed at who shows up to take their place.

How to Not Be a Doormat

Friend, you, too, can run a jackleg-free business. Let me tell you how.

Have Standards, and Stick to 'Em

Write up a list of rules for how you treat your clients and how you expect them to treat you in return. What if a client transgresses, especially if it's something on the smaller side of the scale? The first time, tell that person politely but firmly that you will not be treated like that.

It may well be that the person in question says, "Oh man, I did not realize I was speaking to you in that manner." I have found that many times when somebody unloads on me, it isn't really about me.

I just happen to be the one who's closest to the situation that's causing the client stress in that moment. If you make it clear such behavior will not be tolerated, sometimes the client will apologize for coming unglued. "I honestly did not mean to treat you that way," he or she might say. And after that, the client becomes a great one.

But if he or she turns out to be the other kind? It's time to show that client the door.

Key Takeaways for Banishing Jacklegs from Your Business

Still need some pointers on dealing with this sin? Here's a short list of some of my favorite tricks for installing a handy-dandy "jackleg filter" in your business:

- Stand up for yourself *and* your team. Remember that being a leader means setting a good example and building trust with your associates. That means you don't stand by and let yourself or them take abuse from bad clients.

- If you're forced into a situation where you have to refer one such banished jackleg to another professional in your industry, pick someone you know and respect, and give the fellow a heads-up about the piece of work you're sending along. That way, she won't feel you've sent her unprepared into an ambush.

- Be willing to lose potential income as the price of freedom from an untenable client. Just remember: good money will replace bad money. Yes, it will. Every time!

We're nearing the end of the seven deadly sins of sales. Next up, we'll tackle one of the oldest sins in the book: blowing smoke.

Chapter 7

Sin 6: Cut the Bullhockey (Fluff and Puff)

A Revolutionary Idea

Like most people in the world today, I prefer to shop online before I deal with salespeople. It's not because I don't like them. In fact, it's a joke in my household how easily I will give anyone my money. I research my purchases first because I want to minimize my time dealing with the sales process so I can get on with my life.

When I'm ready to buy a car, for instance, I go on the internet and pick out what I want. I choose all the upgrades I think I need. I'll even email the dealership and text the dealer to make sure the car I want is there before I set a time to go.

Or at least, that's what I did before I met Tony.

I had just come from another lot where I had done my pre-purchase homework, set an appointment to come buy the car I wanted, and shown up, only to discover they'd sold it right before I got there—at exactly the time I'd said I'd arrive.

And what did they say? "Oh, well, we've got this other one instead. And it's on sale!" And they proceeded to sing this vehicle's praises like it had been designed by the Good Lord Himself.

Man, was I torqued. This other car wasn't the same one I'd inquired about and didn't have the features I'd told them I wanted. The salespeople were just interested in moving that car—not in supplying what I needed. Needless to say, I stormed out of that dealership with a still-full pocketbook.

At the next dealership, something miraculous happened: I met Tony. He asked me what I needed, and I told him. If he didn't have it, he said so. And then he either found a way to get it for me or offered other options, which he explained clearly.

It was magical. He even followed up after I bought my Buick from him—a different car, mind you, than the one I'd originally had in mind, but one that turned out to fit my needs perfectly. Tony ascertained this because—get this—he listened to what I wanted, was knowledgeable, and helped me make the right decision.

Ever since then, when I need a new ride, I go see Tony. I know I'll be taken care of and have a good buying experience with no nonsense. In fact, I don't care as much about the particular car as I care about buying it from Tony. Why?

Because Tony is the anti-fluff and puff.

Cut the Bullhockey

The sixth deadly sin of sales is that we are liars. I don't think it's malicious intent most of the time; it's more that we fluff and puff what we're selling. We walk that line between the truth and a lie until, just maybe, we lose track of which side we're on.

However, you already know that if you keep telling lies, the truth is going to catch up with you like that giant snowball that rolls downhill.

All salespeople lie, even just by omission. New-home communities lie about the price by quoting the base-model price and failing to include the eighty-seven upgrades they know you want. The classic used-car salesperson might fail to mention the rust on the underbody, because he or she doesn't expect you to get down there and look for yourself anytime soon.

This situation happens with new homes, cars, insurance policies, you name it. But it has caused people to be immediately hesitant when they need to make a large purchase. Why? Because there are all these *known lies* in the universe!

In the wake of this, a fact that may surprise you comes into play: the best weapon in your sales arsenal is not all that fluff and puff. It's telling the truth.

Because distinguishing yourself from all the lies out there means earning consumers' trust over the long haul, the most successful salespeople you'll meet have learned to cut the bullhockey and tell their customers the truth.

When you're honest with your clients, they feel respected and heard. They know they can come to you with their questions, and they trust the information you give them. In return, they will come back to you time and time again when they need your expertise and refreshing honesty.

If you continue to lie to people, on the other hand, you're setting yourself up for failure. Why is that? It's because now, more than any other time in human history, consumers are highly informed about the products they are buying. That means they are wise to your lines before they even walk in the door. If you start blowing smoke or spouting fake statistics at them, there's a very good chance they'll know you're full of it and walk right back out without giving you the time of day.

Y'all, just be honest with people. You'll be amazed at how much your sales will go up, because once you do right by your customers and pay them the respect of telling the truth, they'll come back to you again— and tell their friends to come see you too.

How to Tell the Truth

Once you realize you'll do more and better business by just being honest, you'll learn there's a right way and a wrong way to tell someone the truth. Here are some helpful tips you can use to guide yourself true.

Know Your Audience

Instead of tossing out industry-insider terms, speak normal language when you're talking to customers. For instance, real estate agents talk about square footage, high ceilings, BRs, and FPLs. But actual humans who want to buy a house want to talk about natural light and usable yard space. Know the difference, and honor what your clients actually want to know about the product you're selling.

Ask Questions

You'll notice this one is a recurring theme in combatting our seven deadly sins, and it's no mistake why. Don't be in "sales mode" all the time. Instead, ask your clients *why* they called you today. See if something in their life changed, or why something you have available caught their eye today when it didn't previously. Ask, and wait for a response. If you're selling something that's not perfect, don't overstate its condition. Instead, ask how the client feels about the exact condition of the item and go from there.

Key Takeaways for Leveraging Honesty

If fluffin' and puffin' is one of your sins, here are some takeaways to post up on the wall in your office so that you don't forget them:

- Today's consumers crave transparency. Instead of sugarcoating a product's flaws, give your clients the pros and cons.

- Always start with something positive. You're still being honest, but kicking the conversation off with something that's genuinely *good* about the product or situation at hand will get things off on the right foot.

- Read *DISCOVER Questions Get You Connected: For Professional Sellers* by Deb Calvert. This insightful take on how to talk to customers offers strategies based on fifteen years' worth of research and anecdotes from actual sales professionals.

We're coming to the end of our seven deadly sins of sales. In the next chapter, we'll cover how to avoid the sin of ignoring a healthy work-life balance by putting the horse before the damn cart already.

Chapter 8

Sin 7: Put Your Horse before the Damn Cart Already (Inverted Priorities)

The Heart of the Matter

I grew up the child of a Realtor®. We had supper every night at 6:30. Our house had a red Southern Bell phone on the wall with one of those double-length cords. If the phone rang during supper, Daddy would get up and answer it and go down the hall to find a place to talk where kid noises couldn't be heard.

When I was on the track team in high school, I decided to throw shot and discus. I became the project of Bootsie Banks, who was a senior when I was a freshman. He patiently taught me how to throw. (I mean, as much as he could. I wasn't exactly a standout!)

If you know anything about track, you know shot put and discus compete at the beginning of every meet. Bootsie was there with me every time, and I'm grateful to this day. But the person I really wanted there was my dad, and I couldn't have him because he was usually out with clients, showing properties in the afternoon.

As an adult, I get it. He was providing for his family in a commission-only job. I understand and value that now. But as a kid, I saw Daddy get up from the dinner table and missed him at my track meets.

When I eventually joined my dad in real estate, I swore I wasn't going to do that to my kids. I wasn't going to do that to my husband, either, because husbands can be very expensive (especially when you make a lot of money).

When it comes down to it, if you aim to honor the clients for whom you work and the community in which you live, you're going to have to honor the special people in your life first. Otherwise, what are we all working so hard for in the first place?

Your Most Precious Assets

The seventh and final deadly sin of sales is inverted priorities, meaning we are guilty of putting our work ahead of ourselves and the people who mean the most to us.

When I speak on this topic, I ask the audience to raise their hands if they've ever skipped or cut short a date night with their significant other for a client. Every time I do, at least 80 percent of the people in the room raise a hand.

Start adding other missed events to that, such as kids' ball games, dance recitals, and teacher's meetings, and guess what happens. Yep. More hands.

The fact that we are willing to shortchange the most important people in our lives for a deal means we have put money in first place. It's easy to excuse ourselves with "Oh, it's just this once." But be truthful. It's *never* just this once.

I get it. Those of us in sales are competitive by nature. And at the end of the day, if you haven't been working, you'll not be eating. That goes for our kids too. But that is no excuse to let your work-life balance get out of whack to the point where it messes up your relationships with the people who make your life meaningful.

Because we strive to honor ourselves and our loved ones in addition to the people and communities we serve, successful salespeople have to learn to draw healthy boundaries around their work-life balance.

I'm not saying that you don't have to make sacrifices to survive in sales, because, well, you *do*. But if you don't create healthy boundaries for yourself, your family will suffer. There's a very high divorce rate among salespeople. Why? Because they work too many hours.

Your health will also suffer. There's a high rate of obesity among salespeople. That's because we don't take the time to exercise. We'd rather spend that time chasing a deal so we can earn more money.

Money is not a good end game. It can never satisfy you, and there can never be enough.

When you do start enforcing healthy boundaries, not only will it improve your health, your general outlook and happiness, and your important relationships, but it will also improve your business relationships.

Your good clients—you know, the reasonable ones you actually want to keep working with—will understand and respect that you have to call them back later because you're at your child's piano recital or with your aging parents at the doctor's office. They'll also respect that you set healthy boundaries and treat you accordingly, making them *great* clients.

If you don't believe me, try it. You'll be amazed to see this really works.

How to Prioritize What Truly Matters

Every time you pick something else over your family, you're setting a precedent with long-lasting effects on your health and happiness, not to mention theirs. To help turn this behavior around, try incorporating the following strategies.

Identify and Honor Your Special People

If you've still got your parents, they are on this list. Significant others and children—also a no-brainer. As for others, maybe it's your grandkids, your best friend, or someone else who's really special to you. Call these people first thing every morning. Tell them you love them and see how they're doing.

Trust me, this will get your day started off right. And it will keep what is most important in life at the forefront of your thoughts, helping you keep your priorities *un*-inverted.

Honor Yourself!

Carve out time in your schedule to do the things that bring you joy. Whether you're married with kids, a single parent, single and carefree, or none of the above, you should still have some hobbies and friends. Everyone needs to blow off a little steam from time to time, and we're all the better for it when we give ourselves this small kindness.

Give Back

Nothing makes you feel more honored than giving of yourself to help others. Get involved in your community by giving your time. Donate a percentage of what you make to the nonprofit charity of your choice, whether that's your church or temple, the local food bank, or any other organization that does important work you believe in.

Key Takeaways for a Balanced Life

If you're about ready to drop this book here and now to charge off to make your kid's soccer game (the one you were going to skip out on a minute ago), here are my top takeaways for a balanced life in a nutshell:

- If you're on your way to church or in the middle of a meal or a special event with your loved ones and your phone rings, don't answer it unless it is actually a matter of life and death. And in sales? That means never.

- Better yet, turn off your phone. Or leave it in the other room or in your car. We are living in a world with luxuries like voicemail and airplane mode—marvelous inventions that give you a reason to stay at the dinner table with your family.

- Make a friend who will walk with you, run with you, or go to exercise class with you. There's no better way to get yourself into shape than having someone else hold

you accountable. (Plus, you can always use
a new friend!)

Now that you've learned the entire litany of the
seven deadly sins of sales, you're ready to take the next
step: giving up your old ways and going from sinner
to saint.

Chapter 9

From Sinner to Saint

The Unstoppable Force

Once you're aware of the presence of the seven deadly sins of sales in your life, you can repent of your wayward ways. You can adjust your strategy and develop the new habits we've discussed in each of the preceding chapters to set yourself to rights. And hey, that's a darn sight better than where you were before!

Even so, continuing to practice those new habits is a lifelong endeavor.

Think of it like playing an instrument. You might be the best pianist in the world. You're traveling the world, performing concerts. Audiences love you. The world is your oyster. But if you stop practicing and learning new pieces, you'll become stale and lose all of the edge that got you to where you are.

Similarly, your choice as a salesperson is simple. You can continually practice the habits you need to stay out ahead of the seven deadly sins and watch your game improve. Or you can rest on your laurels and then one day wake up and realize you've been backsliding again. At that point, you've got to fix the mess you've gotten yourself into (by going back to chapter 1).

However, the more you practice your good habits (dare we say, sales virtues?), the easier they get, and the more fulfilling your work becomes.

When I first started solving the sins in my life, it was out of fear of lost business and a sense that *something had to change.* In changing the way my business was structured, though, I discovered that I also had to restructure my personal life and my approach to clients' needs.

The beauty is that once you address one angle, you can't help but begin to notice if you're off-balance in other angles too. Then you're able to address those issues one by one, and you find out they all work in tandem. A better personal life leads to a more fulfilling sales life, which leads to happier client interactions, which leads back to you having a happier personal life, because now you're dealing with great people who need you and respect you.

And that's something that can make this feel not like a job, but a calling.

Still, when you do find that you've lost some ground, it's time to start practicing and adjusting again. You might even decide you want a little extra help to get yourself back up to a pitch-perfect performance.

And when that happens, you don't have to go it alone.

Your Virtual (and Virtuous!) Sales Coach

If you're ready to take action to stop committing the seven deadly sins of sales, I've got some news for you. It just so happens that there are a lot of people in your shoes, and time has shown us that joining a supportive community of folks who share the same goal is a great way to keep yourself motivated and moving in the right direction.

So, if you need a place to vent, share your stories, and learn about what other people are doing to combat the seven deadly sins of sales, you can visit me on my Facebook page (https://www.facebook.com/NoFluffTraining/) or on my website, the Leigh Brown Experience (http://www.leighbrownexperience.com/). There, you can watch my videos, sign up for my newsletter, join my online training university, and leave me messages. You can also come see me speak when I'm near your town.

Sales can be a lonely business at times, so I am truly committed to helping other sales professionals feel uplifted, inspired, and at the very top of their game. If we work together to keep ourselves and each other on the road to sales sainthood, we can change the way people in our line of work are viewed. And in the future?

There is just no stopping us.

The Future of Sales, Transformed

My wish for you is to see you reshape your sales business by embracing your own humanity and learning how to better communicate with the people you serve.

We can create an entirely new and different experience for the consumer. There are people out there who need to buy right now but feel trapped because they don't want to call a salesperson. This has got to change, and we are the only ones who can change it.

Make your business the type of place people want to call—because they know what that experience will look like before they ever pick up the phone. They have friends, family, and coworkers who have raved about your honesty and transparency and have confirmed that you are, in fact, a real, down-to-earth person with a life and things and people you care about outside of making a buck.

In building this kind of business, you will be changing the popular opinion of what salespeople are like. And before you know it, you'll get a ripple effect that spreads out even further, because when you treat people right, they're much more likely to turn around and do the same to the people they come in contact with day in and day out.

And maybe one day, you'll find that you've established yourself in your community to the degree that you decide to run for public office. Maybe you'll decide you want to put your negotiation skills to good use for the people you share your town, your state, and your nation with. Heaven knows, if salespeople

took the place of lawyers in office, our talent for nego-
tiating peaceful agreements could lead to actual world
peace.

Yep, you heard me. And yes, I do mean it. Sorry,
Miss America.

You're just going to have to find something else to
wish for.

ABOUT THE AUTHOR

Leigh Brown is one of the most successful Realtors® in the country. She is also a forward-thinking CEO, creative author, honest coach, and kickin' keynote speaker. With more than eighteen years of experience in the real estate industry (she started in the biz with her Daddy), Leigh has successfully led her team to be one of the top RE/MAX teams in North Carolina as well as the country. In addition to her impressive real estate career, Leigh is focused on training folks to do better, strive to be more, and to take the reins and lead! Her inspirational speeches have been lauded by audiences around the globe.

Leigh was the National President of the Residential Real Estate Council (formerly known as CRS) in 2017 and is currently an Advisory Board Member for the Realtors Relief Foundation and the Realtor Political Action Committee (RPAC) Chair for Fundraising. She is known for being a sassy Southern woman who is extremely popular for her no-holds barred approach that combines humor with honesty. Leigh lives in Charlotte, North Carolina with her husband, Steve, and their two children, Cora and Timmy.

The Seven Deadly Sins of Sales is Leigh's second book. Her best-selling first book, *Outrageous Authenticity,* can be purchased anywhere books are sold or by visiting www.LeighBrown.com.

Made in the USA
Columbia, SC
17 May 2019